How to Revolutionise Your Relationships

Ephesians

Nicky Gumbel

First published 2008.

ISBN 978 1 905887170

Published by Alpha International, Holy Trinity Brompton,
Brompton Road, London, SW7 1JA, UK.

How to Revolutionise Your Relationships

Ephesians

Nicky Gumbel

Contents

How to Revolutionise Your Relationships

Ephesians 5: 22–33

Wives, submit to your husbands as to the Lord. For the husband is the head of the wife as Christ is the head of the church, his body, of which he is the Saviour. Now as the church submits to Christ, so also wives should submit to their husbands in everything.

Husbands, love your wives, just as Christ loved the church and gave himself up for her to make her holy, cleansing her by the washing with water through the word, and to present her to himself as a radiant church, without stain or wrinkle or any other blemish, but holy and blameless. In this same way, husbands ought to love their wives as their own bodies. He who loves his wife loves himself. After all, no one ever hated his own body, but he feeds and cares for it, just as Christ does the church – for we are members of his body. "For this reason a man will leave his father and mother and be united to his wife, and the two will become one flesh." This is a profound mystery – but I am talking about Christ and the church. However, each one of you also must love his wife as he loves himself, and the wife must respect her husband.

How to Revolutionise Your Relationships

Husbands and Wives

What Paul wrote is as revolutionary now as it was 2,000 years ago. What does it mean to be a Christian? The apostle Paul gives us the answer in the letter to the Ephesians. Calvin described it as the 'Crown of Paul's writings' and the 'Distilled essence of Christianity'.

Not everyone speaks positively about marriage. Abraham Lincoln said, 'Marriage is neither heaven nor hell; it is simply purgatory'. Some people think that if they were married all their problems would be solved. However, someone once said, 'Marriage is like twirling a baton, doing handstands or eating with chopsticks – it looks easy until you try it'.

In this passage from Ephesians, Paul not only tells us how to have a great marriage, but also gives us some tests to use when looking for a marriage partner. Over twenty years ago *Good Housekeeping* magazine published an article entitled 'Six ways to learn everything you ever need to know about a man, before you decide to marry him':

1. *Watch him drive in heavy traffic*
2. *Play tennis with him*
3. *Listen to him talk to his mother when he doesn't know you're listening*
4. *See how he treats those who serve him*
5. *Notice what he's willing to spend his money to buy*
6. *Look at his friends*

And if you still can't make up your mind, then look at his shoes. A man who keeps his shoes in good repair generally tends to the rest of his life too.[1]

The tests given by Paul are somewhat more profound than those offered by *Good Housekeeping* magazine! He asks us to consider whether we could submit to this person, whether we respect them, and whether we love them.

The culture in which Paul lived had a pervading patriarchal ideology. This can be seen in Roman thought as well as in Rabbinic Judaism, where equality for women was unthinkable. Women were regarded as vastly inferior to men. The Greek philosophers in particular perpetuated this thinking.

Plato said, 'A bad man's fate would be reincarnation as a woman'. Aristotle described a female as a kind of 'mutilated male'. He said, 'Females are imperfect males, accidentally produced by the father's inadequacy or by the malign influence of a moist South wind'.

Jesus was born into this patriarchy, and yet he started a revolution. (The term 'Kingdom of God' means 'a revolution'.) Jesus challenged the patriarchy of his day and he challenged the taboo. He spoke to a Samaritan woman in public. He travelled with women disciples. He chose women amongst his closest friends. When teaching about judgment he said 'Two men will be in the field; one will be taken and the other left. Two women will be grinding with a hand mill; and one will be taken and the other left' (Matthew 24:40–42). In other words Jesus said that judgment is not going to be made on the basis of *gender*, but rather it will be made on the basis of *faith*. When he went to dinner with Martha and Mary, Martha was doing what was traditionally considered 'women's work'. Mary took the traditional male role – sitting at Jesus' (the rabbi's) feet. Jesus said, '*Mary* has chosen what is better' (Luke 10:42). Women were the last people to leave the crucifixion, the first to arrive at the empty tomb and the first witnesses of the resurrection.

In this passage, it is clear that the Apostle Paul was following Jesus' teaching about women by challenging the male patriarchy of his day. This passage provides three essential facets for all relationships:

1. Submit in a way that empowers

'Submit to one another out of reverence for Christ. Wives, submit to your husbands as to the Lord. For the husband is the head of the wife as Christ is the head of the church, his body, of which he is the Saviour. Now as the church submits to Christ, so also wives should submit to their husbands in everything' (Ephesians 5:21–24).

The NIV translation of the Bible starts this passage on husbands and wives at verse 22. However, I would argue that the passage should actually start at verse 21. The reason for this can be seen by looking at the two verses in the original Greek:

5:21 <u>υποτασσομενοι</u> αλληλοισ εν φοβω χριστου

5:22 αι γυναικεσ τοισ ιδιοισ ανδρασιν ωσ τω κυριω

The first word (υποτασσομενοι) is translated 'submit'. This word does not appear in the Greek in verse 22. The NIV translates verse 22 as, 'Wives, submit to your husbands as to the Lord...'. This translation is fine providing that it is linked to verse 21, because the Greek literally says 'Submit to one another out of reverence for Christ (v.21). Wives to your husbands (v.22)'. The verb 'submit' is taken from verse 21, and so verse 21 cannot be isolated from 22, because there is then no verb to translate in verse 22. Verse 21 gives us the heading; it is all about mutual submission. 'Submit to one another out of reverence for Christ.'

Paul does *not* use the word 'obey' in this passage. Submission is not the same as obeying. Submission is a kind of deference; a voluntary yielding in love. As Eugene Peterson puts it, 'Be courteously reverent'. Incidentally, note that Paul does not say to husbands, 'Exercise authority over your wives'. Although Paul tells wives to submit to their husbands, the context is *mutual submission*. It is not just a question of who makes the casting vote and who makes the decisions. A husband once remarked, 'I make all the big decisions and she makes all the little ones. Funny how in forty-five years no big decisions have ever come up yet.'

St Paul writes, 'For the husband is the head of the wife as Christ is the head of the church, his body, of which he is the Saviour' (v.23). The Greek word for 'head' is κεφαλη and it can be translated 'head', 'source' or 'origin'. In some places in the New Testament it is probably better to translate the Greek word as 'source' or 'origin', rather than 'headship'. In 1 Corinthians 11:3, for example, Paul is saying that woman originally *came from* man. He talks about women being subject to men, men being subject to Christ, and Christ being subject to God. There cannot be any ontological subordination intended because Christ is not ontologically subordinate to God the Father. This would be a Trinitarian heresy. Christ and the Father are coequal and coeternal.

So what does it mean? There are different views. There are those who believe that the New Testament only advocates male leadership. They point to passages such as 1 Timothy 2:11–12, 1 Corinthians 11 and Titus 2:5. There are others, including myself, who argue that there should be equal opportunities for both men and women to lead in the church. We would point to passages such as 1 Corinthians 4 and in particular to Galatians 3:28, 'There is neither Jew nor Greek, slave nor free, *male nor female*, for you are all one in Christ Jesus'.

This can be understood as a three-stage time bomb. Paul was laying down a general principle that would take quite a lot of time to be activated in history. The barrier between Jew and Gentile came down in the first century, but it took 1800 years to break down the barrier between slave and free. The barrier between male and female has only really come down in the last 100 years, but the foundation for it was laid by Jesus, and subsequently by Paul in the New Testament. In the book, *Does Christianity teach Male Headship?* we read:

> *Just as Paul does not call for a sudden overturning by Christians of slavery and institution, but undermines it from within by urging both slaves and masters to treat each other as brothers in Christ, so too for the sake of social order and successful evangelism he advises the recipients of his letters to go along with some of the social norms of patriarchy even as he proclaims that in Christ 'There is neither... male nor female...'*[2]

There are four key words to remember when considering relationships between the sexes.

(i) Equality

In the creation account we read that when God created human beings in his own likeness, he created them male and female. Paul goes back to the Creation account in verse 31, 'For this reason a man will leave his father and mother and be united to his wife, and the two will become one flesh'. Many translations of the Bible use male language for God, but God's image is represented in male *and* female. God is beyond male and female, although the image of God is represented by the two together. In the Creation account the woman is taken from the man to be his helper. (Sometimes people say, 'Well that sounds like a subordinate role – being a helper'. But this is not the case. The Hebrew word used is the same word used to describe God – God is our helper.) A curse was put on humankind after the Fall, and part of the curse on the woman is that 'He [the man] will rule over you' (Genesis 3:16). This is not *prescriptive* (something that is meant to happen), but rather it is *descriptive* of what, very often, does happen. The dominance of men over women is not part of the creation ordinance; it is a perversion of the Fall. As John Stott writes, 'Without any fuss or publicity Jesus terminated the curse of the Fall, reinvested women with their partially lost nobility and reclaimed for his new kingdom community the original creation blessing of sexual equality'.[3]

(ii) Difference

Men and women *are* different and Paul addresses wives and husbands differently. As John Howard Yoder said, 'Equality of worth is not identity of role'.[4] There are different roles for men and for women. Biologically we know that men and women have been created differently, and of course there are unique roles for women: for example, childbirth and breastfeeding.

We must try to avoid two dangers. The first danger is *gender stereotyping*. The 'men are from Mars, women are from Venus' approach tends to box people in. Not only is it usually possible to find counter examples but, more importantly, this approach is not biblical.

Elaine Storkey writes, '... in the Bible there are no rigidly prescribed roles, no specified division of labour... no stereotypical notions of what it means to be a husband or a wife'.[5] Sometimes people point to The Wife of Noble Character in Proverbs 31, who looks after her husband and her children. However, in the passage we read that she is also the breadwinner for the family, a trader, a property developer and an international businesswoman! It is difficult to use the Bible to support the restriction of women to one particular sphere.

The second danger is to *deny the difference* between the sexes. This suggests androgyny, or ambiguous gender, which is far from what is described in the Bible. God created men and women to be very different. There are beautiful differences between the masculine and the feminine. We get ourselves into trouble when we try to identify exactly what those differences are. Paul does not do that. Instead, he says, 'This is a profound mystery' (v.32), which is much safer. The Bible does not try to restrict the roles, and I personally believe that there is no role that should be denied to a man or a woman in the church because of their gender. When you look at the Bible you see women such as Miriam and Deborah leading Israel. In the New Testament there is an outpouring of the Spirit on both men and women, 'Your sons and your daughters will prophesy' (Joel 2:28). In the New Testament there are women evangelists, women prophets and women deacons. There even appears to be a woman Apostle; in the list of eight prominent women in Romans 16, Junias is listed as an Apostle (Romans 16:7). Ministry in the New Testament is on the basis of gifting, not on the basis of gender. Nobody should be restricted because of their gender.

(iii) Complementarity

'...we are all members of his body'

(Ephesians 5:30).

In 1 Corinthians 12:12–26, Paul speaks about unity in the church, using the image of the head and the body. Though each part is different and performs a particular function, they all need each other. The body needs the head; the head needs the body. It is the same with men and women – they also need each other. Male and female together make up the image of God, and the church needs to reflect that image.

(iv) Union

> *'For this reason a man will leave his father and mother and be united to his wife, and the two will become one flesh' (Ephesians 5:31).*

The one flesh unity that Paul describes here is more than a physical act; it is symbolic of male and female joining back together. Just as woman was taken from man at creation, the unity of the two together represents creation restored. There is a beautiful balance in Paul's teaching.

Should wives submit to their husbands? The answer that Paul gives here is, 'Yes, they must'. The angry refusal to do so, a rebellious attitude, is unbiblical and even ungodly. Should husbands submit to their wives? Paul's answer again is, 'Yes'. Male domination, the arrogance that rules over a woman, is the result of the Fall, and it is not how we are meant to relate. We were not created to relate in that way and it is not how Jesus intends us to live.

John Stott has written:

> *If, therefore, it is the wife's duty as wife to submit to her husband, it is also the husband's duty as a member of God's new society to submit to his wife. Submissiveness is a universal Christian obligation. Throughout the Christian church, including in every Christian home, submissiveness is to be mutual.*[6]

Pope John Paul II's Apostolic Exhortation on the role and dignity of women repudiated a 'one-sided' theory of spousal subordination, and insisted on mutual subordination in marriage.[7] For this reason he called himself 'Papa Feminista' – the Feminist Pope.

This does not mean that men should become weak and wet. The model for submission is Jesus and he is the strongest man, emotionally and spiritually, who has ever lived. There is a need for strong men and for strong women in the church. We see that Jesus' model of submission actually empowers people. Jesus himself submitted in going to the cross. Authority comes from being under submission, and submission is a very powerful word. Markus Barth said:

> *Jesus Christ demonstrates, rather than loses his dignity by his subordination to the Father. When a person is voluntarily amenable to another, gives*

way to him, places himself at his service, he shows greater dignity and freedom than an individual who cannot bear to be a helper to anyone but himself.[8]

Writing about this passage, he says, 'A greater, wider and more positive description of marriage has not yet been found in Christian literature'.[9]

2. Love in a way that endures

'Husbands love your wives...' (Ephesians 5:25).

70 per cent of this passage is about love, and interestingly, it appears to be directed at the man. But is Paul's command to love not also directed at women? Some would say that Paul only tells the woman to submit, and therefore the command cannot be mutual. This is not the case. Just as Paul was talking to both men and women when he tells the man to love; all of these instructions apply equally to both partners in a relationship.

Everybody believes in love, but what does love mean? The kind of love that much of the music industry speaks about is often fleeting. You may remember the old song:

'Hello
I love you
Won't you tell me your name?'

This superficial love does not last. Yet Paul gives us four ways to love in a way that endures:

(i) Enduring love is self-giving

> *'Husbands love your wives just as Christ loved the church and gave himself up for her'*
>
> *(Ephesians 5:25).*

The husband is to submit in the same way that Christ submitted. How did Christ submit?

> *Christ Jesus: Who, being in very nature God, did not consider equality with God something to be grasped, but made himself nothing, taking the very nature of a servant, being made in human likeness. And being found in appearance as a human being, he humbled himself and became obedient to death – even death on a cross!*
>
> *(Philippians 2:5–8).*

Jesus' example gives us a beautiful definition of submission. Submission is the opposite of being self-centred; rather it means being centred on the other.

There are two kinds of people at parties: those who want to go home early, and those who want to be the last to leave. The trouble is that they are usually married to each other! Marriage requires give and take, and as such it requires the giving of ourselves. Tony Campolo, an American sociologist, is visited by many couples whose marriages are in trouble. He says that when he meets with people who are struggling in their marriage, he challenges them by saying, 'If you do what I tell you to do for an entire month, I can promise you that by the end of the month, you will be in love with your partner. Are you willing to give it a try?' He then explains that when a couple accepts his challenge the results are invariably successful:

> *My prescription for creating love is simple: do ten things each day that you would do if you really were in love. I know that if people do loving things, it will not be long before they experience the feelings that are often identified as being in love. Love is not those feelings. Love is what one wills to do to make the other person happy and fulfilled. Often we do not realise that what a person does influences what they feel.*[10]

Self-giving includes forgiving. Jesus gave himself so that we could be forgiven. Ruth Graham (Billy Graham's wife) said, 'Marriage is the union of two forgivers'.

(ii) enduring love is sanctifying

'...to make her holy, cleansing her by the washing with water through the word, and to present her to himself as a radiant church, without stain or wrinkle or any other blemish, but holy and blameless' *(Ephesians 5:26 –7).*

In the USA, one in every three marriages ends in divorce. However, when a couple is married in a church, attends church regularly, prays and reads the Bible together, the divorce rate drops to one out of every 1,105 marriages.[11]

Enduring love should be something that we experience in relationships within the church. The knowledge that you are loved and totally accepted signifies enduring love. Within all relationships there should be a desire for the other's spiritual growth. It reaches its pinnacle in marriage and it enables us to be naked before each other, in terms of being open about our sins, our dysfunctions, our insecurities. Enduring love is a healing power, and this is true in any relationship. Dinah Craik, the nineteenth-century poet and novelist, wrote this:

Oh, the comfort –
the inexpressible comfort of feeling
safe with a person,

Having neither to weigh thoughts,
Nor measure words – but pouring them
All right out – just as they are
Chaff and grain together –
Certain that a faithful hand will
Take them and sift them –
Keep what is worth keeping –
and, with the breath of kindness
Blow the rest away.[12]

As we feel safe with others and are naked before them, we experience the love of Christ incarnated in the community or in the other person. Ongoing relationships in community bring about the healing power of enduring love.

(iii) Enduring love is sensitive

'In this same way, husbands ought to love their wives as their own bodies. He who loves his wife loves himself. After all, people have never hated their own bodies, but feed and care for them, just as Christ does the church – for we are members of his body' *(Ephesians 5:28–30).*

Joan Collins, the actress, was asked how she managed to look so good. She replied, 'I look after myself. I take care of what I eat, I exercise, I tan my body and not my face and I look after my skin *religiously.*' St Paul is saying that now only should we look after our bodies religiously, we should look after our marriage partners religiously, by taking care of their needs.

Relationships are all about nourishing and cherishing, feeding and caring. We feed spiritually with the word of God, and we feed emotionally by communicating with those we love. Communication feeds and then cares. The Greek word for 'cares' literally means 'keep warm'. The word suggests protection, affection, affirmation and encouragement, all of which are of vital importance in all relationships.

Encouragement is absolutely essential in the church. A young woman said to me recently, 'All of my work is discouraging. I am never affirmed'. For 90 per cent of the day she is in an atmosphere with no encouragement. It is only when she comes home, the last ten per cent of the time, that she receives any encouragement. She said that made up for the 90 per cent. We all need encouraging and affirming.

(iv) enduring love is sealed in marriage by sexual union

> *'For this reason a man will leave his father and mother and will be united to his wife, and the two will become one flesh'* *(Ephesians 5:31).*

Robert Spaemann said, 'The essence of marriage is that two whole lives, two whole biographies, are so tied together that they become one history'. That is permanent enduring love. The American pastor, Rick Warren, wrote this:

> *I would be divorced today if it weren't for Kay [his wife] and my stubborn persistence. We said, "Divorce is not an option for us." We locked the escape hatch on our marriage the night we got married and threw away the key.*[13] *We said, "We don't care how miserable we are, we're going to make this marriage work." The night before our wedding Kay's dad sat us down in a room and said, "Kay I love you as a dad and I'll always be here to talk with you and counsel with you when you have marriage problems. We'd like to help you out any way we can. But the Bible says when you marry you make a promise to God and it says a husband and wife will leave their father and mother. That relationship to your parents becomes secondary to your relationship to each other. You are to cleave to each other. Although I love you with all my heart, once you're married you may never come back home." That sounds tough but he was doing it out of love. I am so grateful he said that. It saved our marriage. There are many, many times in those early years when if Kay could have gone back home,*

> *she would have. On the 21 June this year Kay and I will celebrate our twenty-first wedding anniversary. We like to say we've had seventeen great years. The first three years were hell on earth.*

This enduring love is the context for the sexual union; this is the most beautiful view of sex and marriage you will find anywhere in the world.

The sexual relationship is a vital part of marriage.[14] Sex is not the icing on the cake, it is a vital ingredient of the cake itself. Trust and commitment are the bedrock of a good sexual relationship. So often, western culture undermines that concept. We are bombarded with sex everywhere – in magazines, films and on TV. Most films suggest that good sex is about instant gratification with no need for the commitment of a long-term relationship – a beautiful woman and a good-looking man get into bed together and the sex is instantaneously wonderful. But sex is designed for a long-term relationship that can grow and deepen in pleasure and significance as a marriage matures. Sex is a way of communicating love that goes beyond words. It is the ultimate body language. Not only does sex express the one flesh bond but every time a couple makes love tenderly and passionately the bond is strengthened.[15]

Enduring love also requires respect.

3. Respect in a way that elevates

'... the wife must respect her husband'
(Ephesians 6:33).

The word Paul uses for 'respect' is the same Greek word used in verse 21 for reverence, 'Submit to one another out of *reverence* for Christ'. This word can be translated as 'respect' or 'reverence'.

Respect is the key to all relationships. I remember when the Alpha course started to operate in churches outside of Holy Trinity Brompton. We were asked the question, 'Could Alpha work in a deprived, inner-city area where there was high unemployment, low education and low income?' We replied that we did not know the answer. Then a vicar called Eric Delve rang me up and said:

> *We tried it and it worked. I think I know why. It's because of the small groups on Alpha, where people listen respectfully to the views of other people and take a genuine interest in them. The people who come on our course have absolutely nothing. They have no money, no job, and no education. Listening respectfully empowers people who often have very little in the way of power.*

Respect elevates in all relationships.

Respect is key to all relationships between the sexes. We should not get involved in a kind of 'gender war'. Sometimes you see this in extreme feminism or in male chauvinism where there is an enmity between the genders. As Pope Benedict said, 'In Christ the rivalry, the enmity and violence between the genders can be overcome and has been overcome'.

Respect is key when choosing a marriage partner. This is Paul's final test: do I respect everything about this person? Do I respect their character and their views? Do I respect their faith – does it challenge and inspire me? Respect is key to marriage. In verse 33 the respect point is addressed to wives, but it would be absurd to say that is not mutual. As James Dobson put it, 'Respect is intended to operate on a two-way street'. Not just in the first stages of love, but throughout a marriage, because it elevates the other and gives them dignity. Respect increases our confidence and our self-worth.

What about those who say, 'Well, I'm not married and I'm not even thinking about marriage'. Actually, this passage is about you as well. It is about everyone, whether they are married or not. Paul says that he has not been speaking about marriage – he is just using it as an illustration. Marriage is not the be all and end all of life. He uses marriage as a picture of something far more important and long lasting. In this life marriage is fine, but in heaven marriage does not exist. Paul writes, 'I am talking about Christ and the church' (Ephesians 5:32). Marriage is used as a picture of something that is eternal and far more significant: the church. In the Christian community, of which we are all a part (whether we are married or not), will go on forever, and respect is also key to relationships within this community. Therefore, there must also be respect between different denominations, and towards different interpretations of the Bible.

Conclusion

If you are married and think, 'I wish I had a relationship like the one described in this passage', then please consider going on The Marriage Course with your husband or wife. If you are engaged, go on The Marriage Preparation Course. Please read *The Marriage Book* by Nicky and Sila Lee. It is the best book on the subject of marriage that I have ever come across (for more information see the end of this booklet).

If you are looking for a marriage partner (which is a perfectly appropriate thing to do), remember Paul's three tests. Is this the kind of person that I would be willing to yield to? Do we have the kind of friendship that can be an enduring love? Do I respect this person?

The purpose for which you were created is a relationship with Christ. The marriage union is only a picture of the ecstasy of the relationship to Christ in eternity, which begins now. And Paul says, 'That is a profound mystery' (v. 32). The good news is that if you grasp it, it will revolutionise all your relationships.

Ephesians 6:1–4

Children, obey your parents in the Lord, for this is right. "Honour your father and mother"—which is the first commandment with a promise—"that it may go well with you and that you may enjoy long life on the earth." Fathers, do not exasperate your children; instead, bring them up in the training and instruction of the Lord.

Parents and Children

Ephesians 6:1–4

Family life is the foundation of a strong and secure society. Tony Blair, just after he had become Prime Minister in 1997, said this:

> *We cannot say we want a strong and secure society when we ignore its very foundation: family life. ...Nearly 100,000 teenage pregnancies. Elderly parents with whom families cannot cope. Children growing up without role models they can respect and learn from... More truancy. More neglect of educational opportunities... And above all more unhappiness...*[16]

Little has changed since 1997. The subject of family life affects us all, whether you are a parent, or a child with parents still alive, or with parents no longer alive, or whether you are part of the wider family. It affects all those involved with children, not only parents but also those involved in children's church, in schools, in nursing, or social work.

How do we revolutionise our family life? St Paul gives us the answer in this passage.

1. How to honour your parents

Paul's advice to children is, 'Honour your parents...'. Even if our parents are not the best in the world, we should still honour them. When you address a judge in court as, 'Your Honour', you are not making a value judgment about his or her character, but rather addressing him or her with respect for the position. In childhood, our parents or guardians are in a position of authority over us, and that position should be respected. Further, honouring parents is not something that comes to an end in adulthood, rather it is a continuous process throughout our lives. What this looks like in practice changes at different stages.

It is not unlike skiing; there are different stages of skiing with children. The first is when they are skiing as fast as they can, desperately trying to keep up with you. The second stage is when you all ski at the same level, which is great fun. The third is when *you* are skiing as fast as you can, desperately trying to keep up with *them*. The fourth stage is when they do not want to ski with you any more because they are far too good, and they go off and ski by themselves. The fifth stage is when they come back and ski with you because they are so worried that you are going to get hurt! Similarly, there are different stages in the process of honouring our parents.

(i) As a child how do we honour our parents?

As a child, we honour by obeying. Jesus obeyed his parents. We are told that, 'Jesus went down to Nazareth with them and was *obedient* to them...' (Luke 2:51). It is in that context that '... Jesus grew in wisdom and stature, and in favour with God and people' (Luke 2:52). Not only did Jesus grow physically, he grew intellectually, 'in wisdom'; spiritually, in 'favour with God'; and socially, in favour with other people.

Paul gives us three reasons why we should obey. The first is from nature, 'For this is right' (v.1). The second is taken from the Law, a command of God: it is, 'The first commandment with a promise' (Ephesians 6:2). The third is the promise, 'That it may go well with you and that you may enjoy long life on the earth' (v.3). That message is not only directed at individuals, but has a more general interpretation. Strong family life leads to a healthy society.

St Paul does allow for exceptions to obeying our parents in childhood. He says, 'Obey your parents *in the Lord*' (v.1). Children are not required to do things that are immoral or illegal, and the requirement to honour their parents should be followed as far as it is compatible with their primary loyalty, which is to the Lord; to Jesus. This requirement lasts as long as we are 'children'. The definition of this can vary from culture to culture, but in most Western cultures it would tend to be up to the age of eighteen.

(ii) As a young person how do we honour our parents?
First, honour through **friendship**. It is so exciting for parents when their children become their friends and advisers.

Secondly, honour through **forgiveness**. When I look back at my time as a parent I am aware that I made many mistakes. There have been so many instances of weakness, inconsistency, faults and mistakes. Someone once said, 'The trouble with parenting is just the time you get experienced at it, you become unemployed'. Forgiveness applies however bad our parents might have been. It does us no good to hang onto unforgiveness.

Thirdly, **focus** on what they did right. I think this particularly applies if your parents did not give you a Christian upbringing. When I became a Christian my parents were not Christian, and rather than resenting this, I found it so important to focus on what they did right. Though our parents may not be Christians, they may still be very good parents. Blatant attempts to convert them may appear, to them at least, an implied criticism of how they brought us up.

I have three tips for someone in the situation that I was in, someone who becomes a Christian while their parents are not. The first is to be careful of the language you use. I went home and I said, 'I have become a Christian'. Such a direct approach can be quite threatening. With hindsight, it may have been wiser to say, 'I am beginning to find that there is more to the Christian life than I once thought', which is much less threatening. The second tip is to move the focus from your lips to your life. Our parents know us so well and are able to detect immediately the slightest change in our characters. They will be much more impressed by a genuine change in character than in anything we could say. The third tip is to have loving patience. Do not expect dramatic conversions. I have noticed that, of all of my friends who became Christians, within about ten years all of their *parents* became Christians. It did not happen overnight, and they did not have dramatic conversions. Ten years on they were Christians, and they were part of Christian communities, but they might not have been able to say when the change took place.

(iii) As an adult how do we honour our parents?

First, we honour by caring and repaying. In 1 Timothy 5:4, Paul urges children and grandchildren to, '...learn first of all to put their religion into practice by caring for their own family and so repaying their parents and grandparents, for this is pleasing to God'. One of the ways we repay our parents is by gratitude; it is important to let your parents know how grateful you are for their love and support. My own parents were amazing people and I am deeply grateful to them, but I wish I had told them that more often.

The second way we honour our parents is by listening and not despising. Proverbs 23:22 says, 'Listen to your father, who gave you life, and do not despise your mother when she is old'.

The third and final way we honour our parents is by helping and not abandoning them. Jesus instructed the Pharisees to support and honour their parents, rather than claiming that their money had already been given to the Lord. He said that this nullified the word of God, which says that you should honour your parents (Matthew 15:3-6). All the flowers we might give at a parent's funeral are worthless if we did not act in a similar way when they were alive. I remember Bishop Sandy Millar, speaking just after Princess Diana's death. The press had been so rude about her until the day she died, and yet suddenly she had become a heroine. I remember Sandy saying, 'The time to be nice to people is when they are alive'.

2. How to honour our children

Rob Parsons, author and head of the organisation Care for the Family, says, 'No-one should give advice on parenting until their children are at least ninety years of age'. Yet Paul does give advice, and he is speaking in the context of the Roman Empire. What he says is a radical change from the callous cruelty that prevailed in the Roman Empire at that time, in which unwanted babies were abandoned, weak and deformed ones were killed, and even healthy children were regarded as a partial nuisance because they inhibited sexual promiscuity and complicated easy divorce. A Roman father had absolute power over the family. He could sell his children as slaves, make them work in the field in chains, punish them as much as he liked and he could even invoke the death penalty. This power extended through the whole of his life.

It is within this context that Jesus arrives, saying, 'Let the little children come to me, and do not hinder them, for the kingdom of God belongs to such as these' (Mark 10:14). He 'Took a little child and had him stand among them. Taking him in his arms he said to them, "...whoever welcomes one of these little children in my name welcomes me..."' (Mark 9:36–37). 'But if any of you causes one of these little ones who believe in me to sin, it would be better for you to have a large millstone hung around your neck and be drowned in the depths of the sea' (Matthew 18:5-6). He says, 'Have you never read, "From the lips of children and infants you have ordained praise"?' (Matthew 21:16).

Paul follows in the footsteps of Jesus and there are five points we can draw from Ephesians 6:4:

(i) Delight and don't just delegate

Many people like to have children, but not so many like to look after them. In this passage, Paul primarily addresses fathers on the responsibility of bringing up their children. A survey by Cornell University found that the average father spends on average 37.7 seconds talking to his children per day. One third of all children in the United States currently live apart from their biological fathers, and nearly one half live apart from their fathers for a period of three years before the age of eighteen. It is much the same in the UK. We are living in an increasingly fatherless generation. Thankfully, there may be signs that things are beginning to change. There was an article by Kate Muir in the Saturday *Times*, which said:

> *Men of all classes, not just the chattering ones, are recognising the importance of fatherhood.*

> *Why else would Land Rover have created an off-road utility pram? And what of the fine example of England's cricketers, each holding a toddler in one hand and a bucket of champagne in the other, on the Ashes victory tour of London? Men increasingly attend Pampers and parents' evenings, read titles like 'You're Pregnant Too, Mate!', while at the same time finding it harder, as families fragment, to spend as much time as they'd like with their children... Ann Widdecombe says... "It is ironic that now women have fought for the rights in the workplace, men are having to fight for rights to the family".*[17]

Parenting, in an ideal world, involves both parents, mother and father. Because we live in a real and tragic world, this is not always possible, and it is not always someone's fault. When Paul says 'fathers', this can be translated to include mothers as well. The mother's role is a crucial one. Penelope Leach, the childcare expert, recently published a survey of 1,200 children. She found that young children who are looked after by their mothers up to the age of three do significantly better in development tests than those cared for by nurseries, nannies, childminders or relatives. Children cared for by anyone other than their mothers tended to show higher levels of aggression, or were inclined to become more withdrawn, compliant and unhappy.[18] Abraham Lincoln said, 'All that I am, or hope to be, I owe to my mother'.

Paul's letter to the Ephesians guides us regarding our priorities in life. The first five chapters (Ephesians 1:1–5:20) are about our relationship with God, and this is our number one priority. Paul then moves on to husbands and wives, who are considered a higher priority than children. A key element of parenting is to know that the best way to love your children is to love your spouse, and it is very helpful for children to know that the whole world does not revolve around them. Our third priority is our relationship with our children, and they should be a higher priority than our jobs.

There was an interview in the Saturday *Times* magazine with the Hollywood star, Denzel Washington. He has been married to Pauletta for over 20 years and they have four children. He said:

> *Life is family to me. It's very important. You turn up to your son's football game because you want to be there. You want to be with your daughter when she goes skating. Those things are the best things in life. We go to church together as a family and that's a major part of our life, too... Pauletta*

leads all the prayers. She taught the children the prayers and they know more than I do.

A friend was over at our house the other day, having dinner, and we got into this circle to thank God for the food. And he's like, "Oh, this is the latest Hollywood thing?" About four prayers later, after the kids had recited half the Bible, he's like, "Whoa!"

Family is my life and acting is my job.

Denzel Washington has got his priorities right: his wife, his children and then his job.

(ii) Encourage and don't exasperate

King George V said, 'My father was frightened of his mother, I was frightened of my father, and I'm damned well going to make sure that my children are frightened of me'. Yet Paul says, 'Don't be harsh'. What children need is encouragement. Encouragement is like oxygen to the soul.

First, avoid exasperation by affirming our children's dignity. We should not ridicule, patronise, or belittle them. One of the main ways that we affirm people's dignity is by listening to them, and by being genuinely interested in what they have to say.

Second, we should accept their uniqueness. We do this by not setting too high standards or too many rules, and not magnifying minor mistakes. Does it really matter if a teenager's room is just a tiny bit untidy? I recently read a book called *What Every Kid Wished Their Parent Knew – and Vice Versa!* by Rob and Lloyd Parsons, Lloyd being 17 ¾:

> *Dad, I know I can come to you on the meaning of the universe and whether we should join the single currency, but can I ask an easy one? Why is it such a big deal that my room is tidy?*
>
> *Son, that is a really easy one to answer.*
>
> *1. I know it's your room, but it is in the same house as us and plague spreads.*
>
> *2. I think something is moving under your bed.*
>
> *3. We've had complaints from the cockroaches.*
>
> *4. Some of the food under your CD player seems to have turned to penicillin and it's important we get it to people who need it.*
>
> *5. I think the labrador we lost is in there somewhere.*

6. I think something has STOPPED moving under your bed.

7. Some of the underwear in the corner may have come back into fashion.[19]

Third, we should avoid hypocrisy. We must not be inconsistent, but rather let our yes be yes and our no be no. We must admit when we are wrong.

Fourth, we should allow children to develop their independence. One father said this, 'Adolescence is a time of rapid ageing. Between the ages of thirteen and nineteen, a parent ages twenty years'. It does not have to be like that! We have learnt so much from Nicky and Sila Lee, who are experts on the subject of parenting. I highly recommend their parenting book.[20] We go on holiday with their family each year, and each year we are inspired by them. This feeling of being inspired generally dwindles during the year, and then we go on holiday once more and they inspire us again! Nicky and Sila would say that one of the key elements of parenting is not being overprotective. We must give our children space to grow, like a plant. When we first have a plant we might keep it in a pot, but if you leave it in a pot it will suffocate; it needs space to grow.

(iii) Bring them up and never give up on them

The term Paul uses for 'bring them up' is the word for 'nourish' and 'feed'. It is also the word that he uses in relation to the husband and wife relationship, saying, 'No one ever hated his own body, but he feeds and cares for it' (Ephesians 5:29), and we should do the same with our children. The Psalmist says, 'Then our sons in their youth will be like well-nurtured plants...' (Psalm 144:12). We nurture through love; the unconditional love of God. Paul implores us to treat our children in the way that God treats us, which is with unconditional love. We should feed them with attention, appreciation, and affection.

A recent article about the golfer Greg Norman in *Sports Illustrated* magazine commented on his aloofness and cool temperament. Norman explained that he had inherited these traits from his father, 'I used to see my father, getting off a plane or something, and I would want to hug him but he would only shake my hand'. The article described how Norman lost the 1996 US Masters tournament to Nick Faldo, having gone into the round with a six-shot lead. The journalist wrote:

> *As Faldo made one last thrust into Norman's heart with a 15-foot birdie putt on the final hole, the two of them came towards each other, Norman trying*

to smile, looking for a handshake and finding himself in the warmest embrace instead. As they held that hug, held it even as both of them cried, Norman changed just a little. "I wasn't crying because I had lost," Norman said the next day. "I have lost a lot of golf tournaments before. I will lose a lot more. I cried because I have never had a hug like that in my life."[21]

(iv) Discipline and don't discourage

Bring children up in the discipline of the Lord. The writer to the Hebrews says, '... the Lord disciplines those he loves, and he punishes everyone he accepts as a child' (Hebrews 12:6). We need discipline. One of the concerns about the education system today is that there seems to be a breakdown of discipline. A recent incident saw a twelve-year-old schoolgirl needing thirty stitches in her face as a result of a fight in an English lesson. This reflects a real breakdown of discipline in our society. Discipline starts in the home, and it needs to start at a very young age.

Children need boundaries; without them they feel deeply insecure. Life as a child can be like going over a high bridge. I cycle regularly over Chelsea Bridge in London. It is not a particularly high bridge, but there are barriers at each side. If the barriers were not there, I would feel very insecure, and I would want to cycle in the middle of the road. Of course I have no intention of banging into the barriers at the side, but it is a comfort to know that they are there. This is mirrored in an experiment once undertaken by the progressive education movement. One enthusiastic theorist decided to take down the chain link fence that surrounded a nursery school yard, as he thought the children would feel freer without the barrier surrounding them. However, when the fence was removed the children huddled together in the centre of the yard. Not only did they not wander away, but they did not even venture to the edge of the playground.

We all need boundaries. People who are not disciplined as children become very hard to discipline later. It is interesting that in recent years there seems to have been a shift. Not long ago I read an article in the *Sunday Times* stating that, 'Permissive parenting is giving way to the boot camp approach. Even pop stars are at it...'. It went on to describe what one pop star is doing:

> *"Television is poison," says a modern mother in the vanguard of the backlash against permissive parenting. Banned from watching television, her children are allowed a video on Sundays, but if they are 'particularly naughty' they lose this privilege. "If they're just a little bit naughty, then*

no stories before bed," she says. Any clothes they leave on the bedroom floor disappear into a bin bag and have to be 'earned' back by good behaviour. Any arguments over homework mean loss of computer games; and newspapers and magazines are banned from the house. These are not the tactics of just another mother at her wits' end. These are the iron rules imposed by the world's most successful female pop star, Madonna.[22]

We discipline calmly, fairly, quickly, sparingly and clearly. We should discipline, but we should not discourage.

(v) Instruct and don't impose

'... instruction of the Lord' *(Ephesians 6:4).*

The instruction of the Lord involves teaching children to be thankful, unselfish, and good at friendship. Instruction also involves trusting them with responsibility. As parents we must talk to our children about our faith in the Lord, but not force it down their throats. We must try to avoid intensity and simply leave them to decide. It is important to model what we wish them to learn. Someone once said, 'Children have never been very good at listening to their elders, but they have never failed to imitate them'. This is why we have to pray *for* them, pray *in front* of them and pray *with* them. Our hope and prayer is that whilst growing up, a child will be able to say, 'There was never a time when I didn't know the Lord'.

Finally, what really matters – whether we have children or not, whether our parents are living or not – is that we have God as our father. God is the source of all fatherhood. St Paul says, 'For this reason I kneel before the Father, from whom his whole family in heaven and on earth derives its name' (Ephesians 3:14). As John Stott writes:

> *... the true relation between human fatherhood and the divine fatherhood is neither one of analogy ("God is a father like human fathers"), nor one of projection (Freud's theory that we have invented God because we needed a heavenly father figure), but rather one of derivation (God's fatherhood being the archetypal reality, "the source of all conceivable fatherhood").*[23]

Just as marriage is ultimately only a picture of our relationship with God, so too is parenting. Parenting is an image of God's unconditional love for us. As parents we are to model unconditional love to our children, so that they understand that this love is a shadow of what God's love is like.

Kay Warren, the wife of the American pastor Rick Warren, once said this on the subject of parenting:

> *About five years ago when my daughter was going to high school, she wanted to be part of the colour guard team (they work with flags, it's like cheerleading). It really meant a lot to her. She wanted to be on that team. She practised really hard and she went to all of the rehearsals. The day came and she had a great try out and I was really proud of her. But she didn't make the team. She was devastated. All the way home I drove this sobbing, inconsolable girl. There was nothing I could say that would comfort her. She ran upstairs, into her room, walked into her walk-in cupboard and slammed the door. I didn't know what to do. So we decided we'd go and get into the cupboard with her. The four of us, Rick and I and the two boys, went into the cupboard with her. We were all crying and sobbing. After we'd been in there a while, wiping our noses on our sleeves, I said to Josh, "Go and get some Kleenex." After a few moments he came back with one Kleenex and blew his nose. We laughed and the mood was broken. And what had been a tragedy in her life, turned into something that became a shared family experience.*

> *When she and I were talking about it yesterday, she said, "That event, almost more than anything else in my life, cemented for me what our family is. You guys were there for me. You didn't tell me to buck up. You didn't tell me that in the scheme of things this is not that important. You'll get over it. You just got in there and cried with me".*

This is a picture of God's love for each of us. In the story of the Prodigal Son, we read of a father embracing a child, and Paul says that this is one of the main works of the Holy Spirit. The Spirit comes into our hearts to testify that we are children of God; to give us a hug. By the Spirit we cry, '*Abba*, Father'. By his Spirit, we know that we are loved by our heavenly Father.

Ephesians 6:5-9

Slaves, obey your earthly masters with respect and fear, and with sincerity of heart, just as you would obey Christ. Obey them not only to win their favour when their eye is on you, but like slaves of Christ, doing the will of God from your heart. Serve wholeheartedly, as if you were serving the Lord, not men, because you know that the Lord will reward everyone for whatever good he does, whether he is slave or free.

And masters, treat your slaves in the same way. Do not threaten them, since you know that he who is both their Master and yours is in heaven, and there is no favouritism with him.

Employer and Employee

Ephesians 6:5-9

Billy Graham has said, 'I believe that one of the next great moves of God is going to be through the believers in the workplace.'[24] What does that mean for us? In the New Testament, work means more than simply earning a wage. It includes schoolwork, voluntary work, stay-at-home parenting, in fact, any kind of work. For most people, work takes up the majority of the hours that they are awake. Yet many view their relationships at work in a similar way to Tim from the hugely popular television series *The Office*. In one of the more poignant moments, Tim says this:

> *The people that you work with are the people you're just thrown together with. You don't know them and it wasn't your choice. And yet you spend more time with them than you do with your friends or family. But probably all you've got in common is the fact that you walk around on the same bit of carpet for eight hours a day.*[25]

In this passage from Ephesians 6, Paul gives us advice that can have a revolutionary impact on all our relationships at work. Indeed, what he says can transform our whole working environment. Yet we may wonder how a passage about slaves and masters can be relevant to the modern world.

Why did Paul not simply say outright that slavery should be abolished? It is important to remember that at the time of writing, Christians were a tiny persecuted minority who were in no position to abolish slavery. Instead Paul does what he can when the opportunity arises. He writes to his friend Philemon about the runaway slave Onesimus, imploring him to welcome him back as a friend rather than a slave, in other words, 'to set him free'. Nevertheless, as F.F. Bruce points out in *The Epistle to the Ephesians*:

> *To counsel the emancipation of slaves on a general scale would have been to confirm the suspicion of many people in authority that the gospel aimed at the subversion of society. It was better to state the principles of the gospel clearly, and leave them to have their own effect in due course on this iniquitous institution.*[26]

Roman slavery in the first century was not actually as iniquitous as the kind of slavery we might think of, Atlantic slavery, which ended in the nineteenth century. However, as F. F. Bruce points out, 'Slavery under the best conditions is slavery none the less, and it could not survive where the gospel had free course'.[27] Slavery was universal in the ancient world; there were 60 million slaves in the Roman Empire. They were the work force, not just the domestic servants and the manual labours. Doctors, teachers and administrators were all slaves.

The principles behind this passage can still help us today, although they may not be directly applicable. Paul's approach is revolutionary in that he sees work not as hierarchical and functional, as it is so often seen today, but instead in *relational* terms.

1. How to relate to God at work

As we have seen, Paul demonstrates in Ephesians the order that our priorities should take: God is our number one priority, followed by our husbands and wives, then family life, and then, underneath those but above everything else, we find our work. In the church over the centuries there has been a temptation to make a division between sacred jobs, which have been regarded highly, and secular jobs, which have sometimes been regarded less well. There has been a sense that to be a missionary or to work for the church is to hold a 'sacred job' and therefore to have a higher calling. The 'secular jobs' have sometimes been seen as lower callings. Even in secular work we can find a bit of a hierarchy. Perhaps we consider nurses and doctors, the 'caring professions', to be at the top and lawyers and bankers to be at the bottom. However, as A.W. Tozer points out, 'It is not what a person does that determines whether their work is sacred or secular, it is the reason behind it'.[28] It is the motive behind why they do their work.

In this passage, Paul gives us five purposes for work.

(i) Work is worship

'Serving the Lord...' *(Ephesians 6:7).*

The Hebrew word for worship, *aveda*, can be translated either as 'work' or 'worship'. Perhaps the best English word to translate it would be 'serving', in other words, serving the Lord. Paul says, 'Slaves, obey your earthly masters with respect and fear, and with sincerity of heart, just as you would obey Christ' (v.5–6). Paul is saying, 'do your work for the Lord' as an act of worship. Whatever work we do – school work, studying, bringing up children or earning a living – is worship; this makes drudgery divine.

I heard about an American pastor called Howard Hendricks. Once, on an American Airlines flight he noticed that the man sitting in front of him was behaving very badly. Not only was he rude, obnoxious and loud, he then proceeded to get drunk, and became ruder, louder, and more obnoxious. Hendricks was surprised to notice that not only was the flight attendant incredibly dignified when dealing with him, she was also absolutely unflappable. When he was rude, she was polite. When he was loud, she was gracious. When he was impatient, she was patient. Hendricks said, 'I couldn't believe how dignified she was with this obnoxious man'.

After everybody had been served their meals, he got up and walked to the back of the plane to commend the woman. He said, 'I noticed how you handled that man. I was amazed how patient you were with such a rude customer. If you'll tell me your name I would like to write American Airlines, your employer, and commend you for your service.' She smiled at him and said, 'Thank you, sir, I don't work for American Airlines. I work for Jesus Christ.' Hendricks remarked, 'After I picked myself up off the floor this flight attendant started witnessing to me, a pastor! She was telling me I matter to God and he has a plan for my life!'

(ii) Work is minister

'Serve wholeheartedly' *(Ephesians 6:7).*

Although not used here, the very common Greek word that is used in the New Testament for 'serve' can also be translated 'minister'. Throughout the New Testament Paul says that work is ministry. Those who work in the secular world are on the front line. Those of us working in 'the church' are actually just the backup. We are here to equip you for the work of ministry, for what you do in your day-to-day lives. When you serve your boss, your teacher or your fellow employee, you are serving the community. Work in this sense is a practical expression of love to our communities. John Calvin believed that the purpose of work is to strengthen community as an act of love and provision for others. Woodrow Wilson said, 'You are not here merely to make a living. You are here to enrich the world and you impoverish yourself if you forget the errand'.[29]

(iii) Work is rewarding

'... the Lord will reward each one of you'

(Ephesians 6:8).

When we work we are imitating God and Jesus. Jesus said, 'My Father is always at his work to this very day and I, too, am working' (John 5:17). Work is fulfilling.

God was at work when he created this universe. He then created human beings and he put them in the garden to work in it. It was only as a result of the Fall that work was spoiled. We see in Genesis 3 how the ground became cursed and led to painful toil, 'It will produce thorns and thistles for you... By the sweat of your brow you will eat your food' (Genesis 3:18–19). From that moment, no job has been 100 per cent fulfilling. All work has an element of boredom, drudgery and tedium. Yet Jesus came to redeem work, and he himself had a secular job. Work becomes, in the words of the Catechism of the Catholic Church, 'A means of sanctification'. It is one of the ways in which we grow into the likeness of Christ. Work is like sandpaper, shaping us into his likeness, and it is part of restoring creation to how it is intended to be.

(iv) Work is a means of provision

> *'Anyone who does not provide for relatives, and especially for immediate family members, has denied the faith and is worse than an unbeliever'*
> *(1 Timothy 5:8).*

Everybody should get a job if they can at the appropriate time in their life. The only other verse to specifically deal with work in Ephesians says this, 'Those who have been stealing must steal no longer, but must work, doing something useful with their own hands, that they may have something to share with those in need' (Ephesians 4:28). Work is a means of provision for yourself, for your family, and for the needs of others. We are all in it together.

I remember a time when the work of Alpha was growing around the world, and the need to finance it arose. In the beginning, I was very reluctant to ask anyone outside the congregation at Holy Trinity Brompton to help, but it became apparent that the congregation alone could not support it. So, we held an Alpha Partners' dinner to ask people to support the development of Alpha in China, India and various other parts of the world. At the end of the dinner a man came up to me and said:

> *Thank you for this evening. I've been on an Alpha course, my life has been changed and I really want to do something, I want to be involved, but I can't because I'm a banker and I work so many hours during the week, and have a young family to look after. I can't be involved in the running of an Alpha course, but tonight I saw a way I can be involved. Thank you.*

At that moment, it struck me that giving is a way that everybody can be involved in the church community.

The vision of all our churches and charitable organisations could not happen without everyone's involvement. We are in it together and work is a means of provision.

(v) Work is mission

A few hundred years ago, many Christians wanted to go to China, parts of Africa, and other places all around the world where there were unreached people groups. They were keen to be the only Christians in these places. Nowadays, if you want to reach an unreached people group, all you have to do is get a job. The chances are you will be the only Christian in the office, on the shop floor or in the factory. This is an amazing opportunity. It does not mean you have to talk constantly about your faith, which is usually counter-productive. Rather, our faith is primarily about the way we live our lives: our actions; not what comes from our lips: our words. We must live out our faith, and earn a licence to speak. It is no good inviting people to church or to an Alpha course if we do not set a good example in our workplace. When we do a really good job and act with integrity, then people are interested in what motivates us.

I have a friend called Jonnie who is a policeman. He is a relatively young policeman and he is already a Chief Inspector. When he started in his job, he was taught something called 'Locard's Principle', which is used in the detection of every major crime. The principle is this, 'Every contact leaves a trace'. When two objects come into contact with one another, an exchange takes place. When a burglar smashes a window and cuts himself, traces of his blood and fibres from his clothing will be left at the scene. Similarly fragments of broken glass will be found all over his clothing, because every contact leaves a trace. Jonnie realised that this was true not only of his work as a policeman, but also of contact he made with another human being.

2. How to relate to those you work for

There is a book published in the United States by Patricia King called *Never Work for a Jerk*.[30] The problem is that often we do not have a choice about who we work for! Slaves in the Roman Empire had no choice. They could not say, 'I don't like my job, I'm moving'. What happens if your boss is like David Brent from *The Office*? What do you do if you have a bad boss, or a good boss, or just someone in between?

The context of this passage is walking in wisdom, and life in the Spirit. The acronym RECIPE can help us:

'R' is for respect

> *'Obey your earthly masters with respect and fear, and with sincerity of heart'* *(Ephesians 6:5).*

Paul is not talking about servile fear or cringing servility. He is talking about deep respect. He tells us to obey, unless what we are being asked to do is illegal or immoral, or incompatible with the commands of God. This does not mean that as Christians we have to be doormats, far from it. Paul asks us to respect with '*sincerity* of heart' and the word for sincerity can be translated as 'frankness'. I was fascinated to read that one of the values of McKinsey, the world's leading management consultancy firm, is the 'obligation to dissent'. Every employee of McKinsey has an obligation, however junior they are, to say what they think, even if they disagree with someone who is far senior to them. They have a responsibility to express their point of view.

For nineteen years I had the amazing privilege of having Sandy Millar, the previous Vicar of Holy Trinity Brompton, as my boss. There could be no boss in the world better than the now Bishop Sandy Millar! One of the best things about working for Sandy was that he made everything such fun. Noel Coward said, 'Work is much more fun than fun', and certainly that was true working for Sandy. One of the things I always felt obliged to do was to tell him what I thought; it was my responsibility before God. However, once I had told him what I thought, it was not then my responsibility to make sure he *did* what I thought, which would have been disastrous on many occasions! My obligation was to give him my opinion, and then it was his responsibility to decide whether to act on it or not. Once he had decided what he was going to do, my responsibility was to obey him, and to respect his decision.

'E' is for 'excellence'

'...just as you would obey Christ' (Ephesians 6:5).

'Excellence' is demanded because we are serving the Lord. We want to do our very best, just like the airline hostess that Howard Hendricks encountered. Of course we make mistakes. I do not want to criticise the inaccuracies of journalists, but I once read the following quotation, 'Doctors bury their mistakes. Lawyers hang them. But journalists put theirs on the front page'. We all make mistakes. The important thing is that we are consistently aiming for excellence, because the name of Jesus is at stake. We want to be the very best in our field, because we are serving Christ.

'C' is for conscientiousness

'... not only to win their favour when their eye is on you...' (Ephesians 6:6).

We should not work well only when we know we are being watched. We should not be people pleasers. When we are doing our work for the Lord, it does not matter if he is the only person who sees what we do. Charles Spurgeon, the great preacher, once asked a young cleaning woman who had just come to faith what evidence she could now give of being a Christian. She answered honestly, 'I now sweep under the mats'.[31]

'I' is for integrity

'Sincerity of heart' (Ephesians 6:5).

'Sincerity of heart' means uprightness – honesty with our time, with the telephone, with our tax, with truth. There was an article in the *Sunday Times* magazine recently entitled *Naughty Naughty*:

> *Drugs, infidelity, lying to the boss – where do you stand in the modern moral maze? It's never been harder to tell right from wrong. We've gradually traded in the old moral code for one which starts with the assumption that we should all do what feels best for us. The same applies to lying, which*

> *is not okay, unless you are selling a house, or applying for a job, or trying to get out of a social commitment in order to take up a better offer, in which case, anything goes... Basically we've created a whole new layer of behaviour, sandwiched between definitely right and categorically wrong, which is where most people are most happy to operate. In this fuzzy, grey hinterland you can get away with almost anything, provided either you don't get caught, or you turn it into a joke ("I nicked if from the office – it was hilarious!"; "I told them I needed a CAT scan, and they fell for it!").*[32]

I was very struck by a young person in our congregation who started working for a head hunter. One of the first things her boss asked her to do in order to get through to the person she needed to speak to was to lie to the receptionist. She was told it was a necessary part of the job. I spoke to someone else who had worked as a head hunter for some time and asked, 'What does a person in that situation do?' 'Oh', she said, 'It's very simple. I'll tell her the way to get round it. What you have to do is speak to the receptionist with great confidence, you have to get her on your side, and then you tell her the truth! You tell her that you are a head hunter, but you say it so confidently that you get through.' This advice was invaluable. These challenges to our integrity at work can seem insurmountable when faced alone. We need to connect those who are working in the same field with one another so that they can help each other. Those who have more experience can help those who are just beginning. In everything we do in the workplace, we should aim for integrity.

'P' is for passion

'...doing the will of God from your heart'
(Ephesians 6:6).

Though Paul says, '... doing the will of God from your *heart*', the Greek word here is actually 'soul'. We should serve wholeheartedly and put our hearts *and* souls into our work, doing everything with enthusiasm. Ralph Waldo Emerson once said, 'Nothing great is ever done without enthusiasm'. Enthusiasm is infectious; just one enthusiastic person in an organisation transforms the atmosphere. Everyone likes to have enthusiastic people around them, and demonstrating passion and enthusiasm is a Christian duty.

'E' is for expectancy

> *'... because you know that the Lord will reward each one of you'* *(Ephesians6:8).*

Our duty is to do all these things that Paul commands, and then to trust in God for the outcome. Of course, there are disappointments in life. Sometimes we do not get the job we long for. Sometimes we are overlooked for promotion. In these situations, we must know that the Lord will reward us; we must take a long-term view. It can seem that 'career' has become a dirty word in the church today, but it should not be. There is nothing wrong with having a career because God gave to each one of us gifts and talents, and Jesus says that we are to use those talents for good. If we exercise our gifts and our talents, we will progress. Career is progressing in the work that we do, which is a good thing.

What about ambition? Ambition can also be a good thing, but selfish ambition is not. If ambition is just a desire to get rich, to be famous, to be successful, then it is a waste of a life. Jim Collins, author of *Good to Great*, says, 'The top leaders are ambitious – not for themselves but for the company'.[33] They look beyond themselves to the team. As Christians we look beyond our team as well, and we look to Christ. We are ambitious to see Christ's kingdom come, and to see his righteousness. It is a great ambition to want to be the CEO of a company so that you can transform that organisation for Christ.

3. How to relate to those who work for you

In the congregation at Ephesus, slaves were obviously the majority members of the congregation, because they are addressed first and more often, but Paul also addresses the masters in a revolutionary way. In the ancient world, masters did not have responsibilities. They could do what they liked. Yet Paul says, if you are a Christian and you have people working for you, you do have responsibilities. His writing is revolutionary.

Paul says to the slaves, 'Treat your masters as if they were Jesus. Obey them like Christ'. He then goes on to say, '... masters, treat your slaves *in the same way*' (Ephesians 6:9). This is staggering for the time – masters should treat their slaves like Jesus. He illustrates balance to us. The heading of this passage is, 'Submit to one another out of reverence for Christ' (Ephesians 5:21). Paul shows us how that works in marriage, in the parent/child relationship, and here in our workplace. Wives submit to husbands, husbands submit to wives. Children honour your parents; parents honour your children. Those who work for people, treat them like Jesus. Those who have people working for them, treat them like Jesus.

William Shakespeare said, 'O! It is excellent to have a giant's strength, but it is tyrannous to use it like a giant'.[34] Similarly G. K. Chesterton said this, 'There is the great person who makes everyone feel small, but the really great person is the person who makes everyone feel great'.

Responsibility

'... no favouritism' *(Ephesians 6:9).*

Paul is instructing us to avoid discrimination and to treat people fairly for, '... there is no favouritism with God' (v.9). In God's eyes everyone is of infinite value, whether they are slave or free, employer or employee. Everyone is treated well and should be respected in the workplace, regardless of their role or level within a company or organisation.

Release

'Do not threaten them...' *(Ephesians 6:9).*

The Greek word used here means 'loosen'; it means 'unfasten their chains'. We are called to release people. A key attribute of any employer is the ability to help people find the right job, and then release them into it. All of us have different gifts, and there are some things that we are good at and other things that we are not good at. I was very struck reading about Rick Warren, the American pastor, talking about counselling. He acknowledged that counselling is not one of the things that he is good at:

> *I don't think I'm a very good counsellor. I don't have that much patience with people. It's like "Come in. Describe your problem in fifty words or less. I'll give you the solution and you can thank me on your way out." I'm really not into this ten, fifteen weeks of therapy and analysing. I'm not that kind of person. Like, somebody comes in and says, "Pastor, we've got a marriage problem". I want to say, "Why don't you just quit being selfish and grow up! Next problem?" I'm not a very good counsellor.*

As managers, we need to find the right person to do the right job. As soon as we have found that person, we must release them. We must delegate and let them get on with the job. General George Patton said, 'Never tell people how to do things. Tell them what to do, and they will surprise you with their ingenuity.'

In all of this, it is important to remember that ultimately our work does not define who we are. What defines us is our relationship with the Lord Jesus Christ, which is the purpose of our lives. At the beginning of the passage Paul talks about earthly masters, and at the end he talks about our heavenly master, our Lord. More important than our relationship with our earthly employer and employee it is our relationship with our heavenly Lord, this defines who we are.

What matters is that we get our relationship with our heavenly Lord right, and when we do that everything that St Paul talks about in this passage will flow through our lives. We can go out into the world and the workplace and treat people like Jesus. We can be the missionaries. We can be the ministers. As we do that, as we leave a trace on every contact, we will then revolutionise our relationships at work and our workplaces. Then, as Billy Graham said, we will see a great movement of God in the workplace.

If you would like to find out more about the Alpha course, a fifteen session practical introduction to the Christian faith that is running all over the world, please see: **alpha.org**

For more information on The Marriage Course and The Marriage Preparation Course, please see: **themarriagecourse.org**

To find out more about living out the Christian life in your workplace, please see: **godatwork.org.uk**

Notes

1 Lois Wyse, *Good Housekeeping*, April 1985.
2 *Does Christianity Teach Male Headship?* D. Blackenhorn, D. Browning & M. Van Leeuwen Eds., (Eerdmans, 2004), p.21.
3 John Stott, *The Role of Women.*
4 John Howard Yoder, *The Politics of Jesus*, (Doubleday, 2006), p.177, footnote 23.
5 Elaine Storkey, *What's Right with Feminism?* (Revised Ed. SPCK 2006), p.171.
6 John Stott, *The Message of Ephesians: God's New Society*, (IVP, 1991), p.233.
7 Mulieris Dignitatem
8 Markus Barth, *Commentary on Ephesians, Volume 2* (Doubleday, 1974), p.714.
9 Markus Barth, *Commentary on Ephesians, Volume 2* (Doubleday, 1974), p.715.
10 Anthony Campolo, in *Homemade*, June 1988.
11 *Marriage and Divorce Magazine*, March 24, 1980.
12 Dinah Craik, *A Life for a Life*, 1859.
13 There are situations where this would not apply, for example in cases of domestic violence or abuse.
14 Of course, there may be situations in marriage where the sexual relationship cannot continue, for reasons such as disability or illness.
15 For more about the sexual relationship within marriage, please see, Nicky and Sila Lee, *The Marriage Book*, (Alpha International, 2002).
16 Tony Blair, Labour Party Conference, Brighton, Tuesday 30 September, 1997.
17 Kate Muir, Saturday *Times*, 24 September, 2005.
18 The *Times*, 3 October, 2005.
19 Lloyd & Rob Parsons, *What Every Kid Wished Their Parents Knew ... and Vice Versa*, (Hodder & Stoughton, 1999).
20 Nicky & Sila Lee, *The Parenting Book*, (Forthcoming, Alpha International).
21 *Sports Illustrated*, 30 December, 1996.
22 Lois Rogers and Zoe Brennan, *Sunday Times*, 16 October 2005.

23 John Stott, *The Message of Ephesians: God's New Society*, (IVP, 1991), p.134
24 John C. Maxwell & Stephen R. Graves, *Life@Work Handbook*, (Thomas Nelson, 2005).
25 Ricky Gervais & Steven Merchant, *The Office*, Episode 3.01.
26 F.F. Bruce, *The Epistle to the Ephesians*, (Eerdmans USA, 1957).
27 F.F. Bruce, *The Epistle to the Ephesians*, (Eerdmans USA, 1957).
28 Quoted in John C. Maxwell & Stephen R. Graves,. *Life@Work Handbook*, (Thomas Nelson, 2005), p.122.
29 Quoted in John C. Maxwell & Stephen R. Graves, *Life@Work Handbook*, (Thomas Nelson, 2005), p.67.
30 Patricia King, *Never Work for a Jerk*, (Franklin Watts, 1987).
31 Mark Greene, *Thank God It's Monday*, (Scripture Union, 2001), p.103.
32 Shane Watson, the *Sunday Times* Magazine, 30 October 2005.
33 Jim Collins, *Good to Great*, (Harper Collins, 2002).
34 William Shakespeare, *Measure for Measure*, Act 2: Scene 2: 133-5.